EDGE OF MEDICINE

VACCINE

BREAKTHROUGHS

T0015961

HEATHER E. SCHWARTZ

MAYO CLINIC PRESS KIDS

To Philip, Jaz, and Griffin

MAYO CLINIC PRESS KIDS | An imprint of Mayo Clinic Press
200 First St. SW
Rochester, MN 55905
mcpress.mayoclinic.org
To stay informed about Mayo Clinic Press, please subscribe to our free e-newsletter at mcpress.mayoclinic.org or follow us on social media.

For bulk sales to employers, member groups and health-related companies, contact Mayo Clinic at SpecialSalesMayoBooks@mayo.edu.

Proceeds from the sale of every book benefit important medical research and education at Mayo Clinic.

ISBN: 978-1-945564-73-4 (paperback) | 978-1-945564-74-1 (library) | 978-1-945564-76-5 (ebook) | 979-8-88770-091-5 (multiuser PDF) | 979-8-88770-092-2 (multiuser ePub)

Library of Congress Control Number: 2022942503
Library of Congress Cataloging-in-Publication Data is available upon request.

TABLE OF CONTENTS

VACCINE
SALVATION

In December 2019, people in China began falling ill and dying. They were victims of a new and highly **contagious** virus. By early 2020, the virus swept the globe, with new waves erupting again and again. Daily life came to a standstill.

Thousands, and then millions, of people died from the SARS-COV-2 virus. Scientists labored to understand the new virus and end its spread. They were in a race against time. Could a vaccine help end the **COVID-19 pandemic**?

COVID-19 was not the world's first pandemic. Diseases have plagued humans for centuries. But time and again, vaccines tamed these outbreaks. The invention of vaccines has transformed history and saved lives.

Today, vaccines are tested and approved to protect against many illnesses. Even after approval, they're continually tested and **monitored** to make sure they're safe and highly effective. Some vaccines have even **eradicated** widespread, deadly diseases!

US toddler Will Maddock and his mom pump their fists in victory to celebrate Will receiving the COVID-19 vaccine in 2022. Will's heart defect meant catching COVID-19 could be deadly.

THE WORLD'S
FIRST VACCINE

In the 1700s, smallpox was the top cause of death in Europe. Nothing people tried slowed smallpox deaths. Then British doctor Edward Jenner noticed something. He realized people who previously had the milder disease cowpox didn't seem to catch smallpox. This gave him an idea. Jenner began to experiment.

In 1796, Jenner visited a woman who was sick with cowpox. He removed **pus** from one of her sores created by the disease. Jenner **injected** this pus into a healthy boy. The boy developed cowpox, as Jenner expected. After mild symptoms, the boy recovered.

It was time for the second part of Jenner's experiment. He injected the boy with smallpox. But the boy remained healthy! He did not develop smallpox. This proved what Jenner had hoped. An injection of cowpox prevented **infection** by smallpox. Jenner had invented the world's first vaccine!

The smallpox vaccine eradicated the disease. And it may be the solution to a newer disease too. In 2022, a virus called monkeypox broke out in the United States. Scientists learned the virus was similar to smallpox. They discovered Jenner's vaccine could also protect against monkeypox!

Edward Jenner injects eight-year-old James Phipps with smallpox in 1796. Phipps was the son of Jenner's gardener.

DISCOVERING ATTENUATED VACCINES

In the late 1800s, French scientist Louis Pasteur was inspired by Jenner. Pasteur began experimenting using infectious agents to protect against disease, as Jenner had.

In 1884, Pasteur and his student Emile Roux broke new ground with a new kind of patient—dogs! They injected 50 dogs with live rabies virus. Pasteur and Roux attenuated, or weakened, the rabies first. They hoped weakening the virus would allow the dogs' bodies to fight it and develop **immunity** to it.

Months later, Pasteur and Roux injected the dogs with rabies virus that had not been weakened. The dogs remained healthy! The experiment worked. But would it work for people? Pasteur felt it was too risky to test.

Then, in 1885, Pasteur learned of a boy who had recently been attacked by a rabid dog. If the boy got rabies, he would die.

By 1885, Louis Pasteur had immunized 50 dogs against rabies.

Pasteur injected the boy with his live attenuated vaccine. As Pasteur predicted, the boy did not develop rabies! The boy was the first person injected with an attenuated virus.

Attenuated vaccines changed the field and saved many lives. In the following century, scientists used attenuated vaccines to prevent measles, mumps, rubella, chicken pox, and more.

MODERN MIX
DEFENDS KIDS

Until the early 1920s, **diphtheria** was the top cause of death amongst children worldwide. Parents lived in fear of the disease. Today, a vaccine made for children prevents diphtheria. The vaccine's formulation was the first of its kind.

German scientist Emil von Behring began studying diphtheria in the 1880s. For years, he tried and failed to inactivate the **toxin** that caused the disease. He took a new approach in 1901.

Von Behring mixed two elements. The first was weakened toxin. The second was an **antitoxin**. This was blood extracted from a horse that had caught diphtheria and developed **antibodies** to fight it. Von Behring believed the combination of these elements would give a patient the disease along with a weapon—the antibodies—to fight it. He was right!

After years of development, the diphtheria vaccine was created in the 1920s. By the 1930s, it was a regular part of childhood medical care. To parents' relief, cases of diphtheria dropped dramatically.

A late 1930s or early 1940s advertisement urges parents to vaccinate their children with the diphtheria toxoid. *Toxoid* is the term for a purified preparation of a toxin.

COMBINED VACCINES
SAVE MORE LIVES

By the 1940s, the public understood that vaccines kept them healthy. But they did not enjoy getting injections! Fear of needles made some people avoid getting vaccines. Others skipped vaccines due to the inconvenience of needing several appointments for many different shots.

Scientists wanted to make vaccination more accessible. They began formulating one shot that would be able to **deliver** several vaccines at once. In 1948, US doctors Pearl Kendrick and Grace Eldering succeeded. They combined vaccines for diphtheria, tetanus, and pertussis (whooping cough) into one shot, called the DTP. This vaccine was the first of its kind. Today, formulations of this vaccine, now called DTaP and Tdap, are given and save millions of lives each year.

In 1971, US scientist Maurice Hilleman followed Kendrick and Eldering's example. Hilleman combined the vaccines for measles, mumps, and rubella (MMR) into one shot. Making it easier to get all three vaccines, the MMR vaccine prevented millions of deaths.

Many vaccines, including the DTaP, are given to babies under age one. Combining vaccination for several diseases reduces the number of painful shots children must receive.

NEEDLE-FREE
VACCINATION ARRIVES

Combined vaccines allowed people to receive more vaccines with fewer shots. But it did not solve patients' fear of needles. This fear is especially common in children. Vaccinations can be emotionally difficult for the kids receiving them, their caretakers, and the medics administering them. Medical researcher Albert Sabin changed that in 1961.

Since the 1940s, polio outbreaks had killed thousands of children each year. In 1955, scientist Jonas Salk created a polio vaccine that slowed polio outbreaks. But the vaccine required several shots. Sabin wanted to provide an easier, pain-free way to vaccinate children.

In 1961, Sabin created a liquid vaccine that was dropped into a beverage or on a sugar cube, which could then be ingested. Parents raced to get their children this easy-to-take **oral** vaccine. Sabin's work pushed Salk's into overdrive. Together, they eradicated polio.

A Texas woman holds her two-year-old son as they both take a Sabin polio vaccine sugar cube in 1962.

Another Salk creation, the flu vaccine, was given a pain-free update in 2003. That year, health officials approved a **nasal** spray flu vaccine created by Syrian doctor Hunein Maassab. The nasal spray provides kids and anyone afraid of needles pain-free protection from the flu.

NIPUNIE S. RAJAPAKSE, MD, MPH
MAYO CLINIC

Q: What do you like best about treating children?

A: I love being a doctor for children because they are so strong and resilient! My patients inspire me every day. It is so rewarding to take care of a child who may have been very sick and had to stay in the hospital for a long time and then see them going back to school and playing sports and doing all the other things they enjoy. Kids' bodies are so amazing in their ability to heal and recover from illness or injuries—they do this better than most adults!

Q: What do you wish more people knew about vaccines?

A: I wish people knew more about how carefully vaccines are studied and monitored to make sure they not only work well but are also very safe! There is a lot of misinformation about vaccines out there and this results in people not getting vaccinated which leads to many outbreaks, illnesses, and even deaths which could have been prevented.

Q: Why does your arm hurt after getting a vaccine?

A: When your arm hurts after getting a vaccine it is a sign that your **immune system** is doing its job and building protection against the infection(s) you were vaccinated for. The pain is caused by inflammation which comes from your immune system responding to the vaccine. Inflammation can sometimes cause some redness or swelling as well. Some of the pain can also be due to stretching of your muscle fibers from the small amount of fluid that is injected.

Q: Why is it important to get vaccines?

A: Vaccines allow our bodies to develop protection against many infections without having to get sick with the infection itself. When we keep our vaccines up to date, we are not only protecting ourselves but also the people around us because we are less likely to get sick or spread the infection to others. This is especially important for the protection of people who might not be able to get vaccinated themselves, for example because they are too young or have a weakened immune system.

Q: Can you get sick from a vaccine?

A: Vaccines can sometimes cause side effects like fever, tiredness, or muscle aches and pains. You might even feel like you have the flu! These symptoms are usually mild and resolve over the course of a couple of days without any long-term effects. Even though you may not feel great, these symptoms are actually a good sign your immune system is hard at work doing its job to respond to the vaccine and provide you with protection from the infection(s) you were vaccinated against.

Children can begin receiving vaccines as young as two months of age. Vaccines protect against many diseases that have no cure. Getting vaccinated against these diseases at a young age provides early protection.

PREVENTS CANCER

Past research helps scientists develop modern vaccines. But they also have to answer new questions as they work. In the 1990s, scientists studied the human papillomavirus (HPV). They knew previous vaccines worked by introducing a weak **strain** of a virus into the body. But that was too risky with HPV. Research had shown even a weak strain of HPV could cause cervical **cancer**. Scientists had to find another way to prevent this disease.

US doctors Doug Lowy and John Schiller created virus-like particles to use instead of actual HPV. The particles were shaped to be similar to HPV **virions**. When the particles are injected into a patient, their body reacts to them as though they are HPV. This stimulates their body to produce antibodies to fight the disease. So, the patient develops protection to HPV without being exposed to it!

The HPV vaccine came out in 2006. It prevents more than 30,000 cases of cancer in the United States each year.

Antibodies (*green*) latch onto virus-like particles (*yellow*) that are similar to HPV virions and have attached to cells. The antibodies will automatically fight any future particles that resemble this shape!

MYSTERIOUS
ANTIBODY LINK?

The first Ebola outbreak was in 1976, in West Africa. Since then, the deadly, highly infectious disease has caused thousands of deaths worldwide. Scientists sought prevention of Ebola for decades. In 2019, they succeeded. That year, manufacturer Merck released an Ebola vaccine.

Merck scientists added an Ebola **glycoprotein** to vesicular stomatitis virus (VSV) as a safer way to study Ebola. Though VSV is a virus, it does not cause illness in people. The scientists learned that when Ebola is attached to VSV, it doesn't cause infection either. But VSV *does* ignite the body's **immune response**. When combined in a vaccine, the body recognizes and then fights the injected virus, including the Ebola connected to it.

Malaria is an equally deadly and infectious disease. And like Ebola, its vaccine took decades to develop. The **parasite** causing malaria changes after infection. A vaccine that works while the parasite is in one stage will not work when it reaches the next.

After more than 30 years studying the disease, researchers developed a malaria vaccine in 2021. The vaccine triggers the immune system when the parasite is in its first stages. Researchers predict it could save the lives of 23,000 people each year.

Research on both diseases also found a link in 2019. People with active and recent malaria may have antibodies against Ebola. Could this link lead to new vaccines?

Medical workers wear protective gear while handling Ebola samples. Ebola is transmitted through direct contact with blood, or any other bodily fluids, infected with the disease.

COVID-19 VACCINE:
GLOBAL RELIEF

By August 2021, COVID-19 had altered global daily life for more than a year. But when the COVID-19 vaccine was authorized that month in the United States, some people refused it. They felt it was developed too quickly. It is the first vaccine to use **messenger ribonucleic acid** (mRNA) technology. How was it possible scientists had created a cutting-edge, effective vaccine in under two years?

In reality, scientists had been working on vaccines to prevent coronaviruses decades before COVID-19 **emerged**. They had also been researching mRNA. In the body, mRNA is like a recipe. It carries instructions to cells, telling them how to make **proteins**. Scientists felt this process might be useful in vaccines. They just needed to figure out how. In 2021, US scientists Katalin Karikó and Drew Weissman figured it out.

Karikó and Weissman found that mRNA could be used to tell cells to produce spike proteins. These spikes resemble those found on a SARS-COV-2 virus cell. The body recognizes

Many COVID-19 vaccines were administered in drive-throughs, with patients remaining in their cars. This was to avoid bringing possible germs indoors, and to accommodate the large numbers of people rushing to get the vaccine once available. Some clinics vaccinated thousands of people each day in 2021!

the spikes as **foreign** and fights them. It also remembers the spikes and, if necessary, will be ready to block the real, similarly shaped SARS-COV-2 spikes in the future. This is how Karikó and Weissman's vaccine works!

The scientists' breakthrough became the foundation for the COVID-19 vaccine. Some people remained unsure of the new technology. But the vaccine was developed using research and trials to make sure it was safe.

The COVID-19 vaccine saved nearly 20 million lives in the first year. People could move forward without so much fear of catching the disease. And scientists had a new discovery to build on. Work on the COVID-19 vaccine could lead to many more mRNA vaccines for other infectious diseases, for cancer, and even for certain allergies!

HOW MRNA WORKS IN THE COVID-19 VACCINE

1 The vaccine contains mRNA packets in lipid nanoparticle.

2 mRNA enters the cell. Instructions for making spike proteins are passed to the cell.

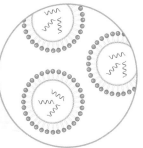

3 The cell makes proteins that leak out of the cell and create spikes.

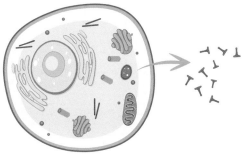

4 White blood cells recognize spike proteins and make antibodies.

5 Antibodies attach to the virus and block it from infecting cells.

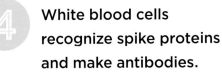

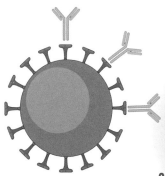

TIMELINE

1796

The world's first vaccine is invented to prevent smallpox.

1901

A pediatric diphtheria vaccine is developed.

1885

A test of the rabies vaccine on a human patient proves successful. This proves attenuated vaccines can be safe and effective.

1948

The first combined vaccine protects against diphtheria, tetanus, and pertussis. Protection against all three diseases becomes easier, with modern formulations saving millions of lives each year.

1961

The oral polio vaccine is developed. It's easier for children to take, leading to higher vaccination rates and the eradication of polio.

2006

Scientists develop the HPV vaccine. It uses a mock virus to prevent cancer.

2019

The Ebola vaccine is released. It uses vesicular stomatitis virus to trigger an immune response.

2003

The nasal spray flu vaccine is approved. It provides patients who are afraid of needles pain-free flu protection.

2021

The malaria vaccine is released. It stops the malaria parasite in its early stages.

The COVID-19 vaccine is approved. It's the first vaccine to use mRNA technology.

GLOSSARY

antibody—a substance produced by the body to fight disease

antitoxin—something that counteracts a toxin

cancer—a group of often deadly diseases in which harmful cells spread quickly

contagious—spread through direct or indirect contact

COVID-19 pandemic—a global spread of the SARS-COV2 virus beginning in early 2020

deliver—to send or bring

diphtheria—an infection caused by bacteria that make toxin, and which can lead to difficulty breathing, heart problems, and death

emerge—to appear after being newly created or having grown in strength or popularity

eradicate—to completely destroy or put an end to

foreign—something that is not a part of, or is from outside, the body

glycoprotein—a protein with sugar molecules attached to it

immune response—how the immune system reacts to changes or foreign objects

immune system—the system that protects the body from diseases

immunity—resistance or protection from an infection or disease

infection—the entrance and growth of germs in the body. Being capable of creating and spreading infection to others is called being infectious.

inject—to force a liquid medicine or drug into someone using a special needle. The medicine received is called an injection.

messenger ribonucleic acid—molecules that carry the genetic information the body needs to make proteins

monitor—to watch or keep track of

nasal—of or relating to the nose

oral—of or relating to the mouth

parasite—an animal or plant that lives in or on another animal or plant and gets food or protection from it

protein—a molecule of amino acids that is essential to body function

pus—a thick liquid produced by tissue infected with certain diseases

strain—a genetic virus variant that is built differently, and so behaves differently, than its parent virus